COMPOSTING

COMPOSTING

·Bob Flowerdew·

Kyle Cathie Limited

First published in Great Britain in 2010 by
Kyle Cathie Limited
23 Howland Street
London, W1T 4AY
www.kylecathie.com

Text 2010 © Bob Flowerdew
Design 2010 © Kyle Cathie Limited
Photography 2010 © Peter Cassidy
Illustration 2010 © Alison Clements

ISBN 978-1-85626-930-8

10 9 8 7 6 5 4 3 2 1

A Cataloguing in Publication record for this title
is available from the British Library.

Photography: Peter Cassidy
Illustrations: Alison Clements
Design: Louise Leffler
Project Editor: Sophie Allen
Copy Editor: Helena Caldon

Photographic Acknowledgements:
All photography by Peter Cassidy except
pp. 9, 57 by Bob Flowerdew

Printed in China by 1010 Printing International Ltd

Contents

Introduction

Compost is magical stuff – much like well-rotted farmyard manure but cleaner and sweeter, more like rich friable loam. And it has a host of benefits. Indeed, the more compost is investigated, the more benefits are found. Applying compost feeds your soil, helps conserve moisture, then feeds your plants and simultaneously controls many pests and diseases. Yet it is but the rotted down remains of our kitchen and garden wastes. Stuff that otherwise would be a problem and would cost to get rid of.

Making and applying compost is an essential for organic gardeners, but it is good sense for everyone else, too. Nothing you can do in the garden gives as many returns as collecting materials and mixing them into a compost bin. The health, vigour, yield and taste of your plants all improve and you benefit from eating the nutrient-rich produce that grows from it. Not only will you recycle your wastes; probably soon you will be scavenging from others and helping to clean up a messy world. Even weeding, mowing and hedge trimming become less arduous when you realise what valuable nutrients they contribute to your compost bin.

I am fascinated by composting; how different mixtures of all sorts of things come out as such a uniform and useful product. I have been composting for three decades and I have tried many methods. What is amazing is that, given a few basics, composting always works so well and produces such excellent results. Even badly made compost has a use, indeed, left much longer it would eventually become better compost. However, with careful mixing in a decent container good compost can be made in only a matter of months. Be warned, though; once you find out how effective and useful compost is there is never enough.

Why compost?

We're all composting nowadays. Most of us compost because we want to, but some because there is no other legal easy way of disposing of household and garden wastes. Apart from being such a simple solution, composting has another benefit worth having. In decomposing the raw materials a compost bin creates fertility, something you would have to buy in otherwise. Compost is a natural fertiliser and soil enricher that feeds your garden better than any bought-in fertiliser, and does as much good as a whole load of well-rotted manure. For compost does not just feed the soil immediately but also inoculates it with micro-organisms that liberate the soil's locked-up wealth of nutrients. Compost in the soil degrades and becomes humus, which benefits the soil by improving its crumb structure, multiplying the water-holding capacity, and darkening the soil so that it warms up more in the sun. All this from wastes that would otherwise be sent to landfill (costing us money to transport them there), where they would slowly decay giving off atmosphere-destroying gases whilst leaching residues into our drinking water. Whereas a proper compost heap lets little of value escape, capturing it all to be returned as fertility for healthier plants and bigger crops. Even just having a compost heap encourages wildlife in your garden. Vast numbers of small critters

Right: Not rubbish but treasure...

live in, around and especially underneath compost bins. These in turn bring in more attractive creatures, such as hedgehogs and birds. So your garden wins in many ways, and all for free. Remember, composting is a natural process, and even if it does go a bit wrong it can always be put right again, and no innocent lives are lost – in fact, countless billions are born hourly in every bin!

Food for thought

Here's some food for thought: organisms in healthy soil need but a small addition of compost annually to help them combine minerals, water and air to create natural fertilisers which will feed and fatten plants. Figures suggest that somewhere between a quarter to half of all food produced is not eaten but thrown away. If it were returned to the farmers and composted, it could be enough fertility to grow much of our food for the following year.

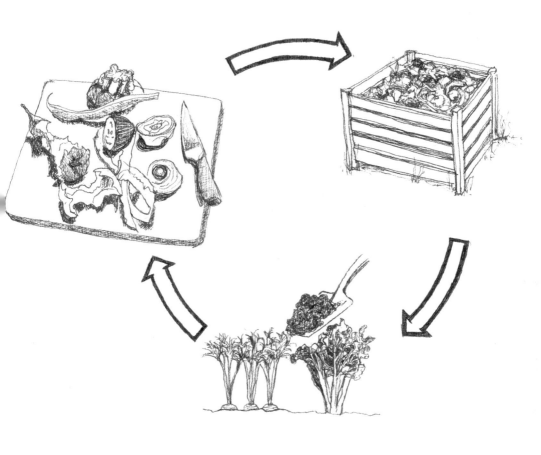

'There are no more weeds, wastes or surplusses;
they have all become pieces of future fertility.'

When did composting begin?

The deliberate construction of actively decomposing compost heaps for their soil-enhancing and enriching product is a relatively recent introduction to Western gardening. On the other side of the world, clever composting processes have long been employed by the Chinese, but their use rarely spread outside their region.

Perhaps the earliest pioneers copied nature, which gives us examples of natural composting. Falls of leaves and other matter accumulate in holes and against banks and hedges, and piles of dung build into heaps as animals return to the same 'toilet'. As early humans settled here and there, they left archaeologists treasure troves of their kitchen middens. These, the remains of all their household wastes, were lazily dumped near their dwellings. With civilisation, the wastes became deposited further from the house, though, at best, just outside the town or city walls. The fertility of these piles of rotting materials must have been evident from the vigour of the plants that sprang from seeds consigned to these dumps.

Anyhow, somehow from ancient times it was known that muck heaps and other decayed materials fed the soil. Perhaps it was because these middens would someday have been levelled for other purposes and then most likely spread on the fields, and the resultant lush

Right: All of this will, eventually, rot and disappear into the soil

growth here and there would have been noted. The realisation grew that piles of nastiness, if left long enough, broke down into something less nasty to handle and somehow this helped the crops. (Gifts of 'decayed food' to the gods of the fields may not have been far removed in their psyche from animal or human sacrifice, which would also have been seen to stimulate following crops. Indeed, dried blood is still sold as one of the quickest fertilisers to act.)

So, returning our wastes to the soil is not new. Everything from bones, woollen shreds, fire ashes and pottery shards were routinely spread on the fields. However, most probably this was as often simply to get rid of smelly stuff as for improving fertility. Little was deemed valuable enough to be moved far from its source, and no effort was made to combine these wastes to reform them into a far more valuable compost.

Deliberately made composting heaps seem not to have been made intentionally to enhance soil fertility, but once it was noticed how rain could leach away the goodness on Roman farms, efforts were occasionally made to cover dunghills and to recycle any run-off. Eventually, during the Renaissance, others noted how chance or careful mixing could cause a heating and more rapid decomposition. This was then employed to make hot beds on which earlier and out-of-season crops could be forced, and in France this heating was used to make a semi-sterilised soil suitable for mushroom growing. In Victorian times, the expensive and soon dwindling imports of guano (fossilised bird manure), bones, mineral and natural fertilisers had experimenters trying all sorts of specialised composting processes to try and convert everything possible into new wonder fertilisers. But with a few exceptions that's all they were trying to create; a chemical fertiliser of incredibly high nutrient value, not a micro-life-enhanced, catalytic soil enricher and health promoter. This is now seen as the primary role of compost for plant and food health; adding compost to your soil is not just to feed your plants but also to protect them from many foes, both directly and indirectly.

The creation of the 'modern' compost heap, with its use of compost as a catalyst for soil, plant and animal health, seems to have originated with Sir Albert Howard's Indore method (please note: regardless of pronunciation, this comes from his experimental work in Indore in India, not Indoor) and the works of Maye E. Bruce and F. C. King. The rise of the Organic (and the continental parallel, Bio-dynamic) method of gardening and farming introduced many more people to the undoubted horticultural benefits of using compost. But the biggest impetus was given by outside factors. Two world wars made chemical fertilisers expensive; the restricted availability of manures, and then doubts about contamination in those manures, made many reluctant to use them. Since then, a growing awareness of the importance of soil life and ecology, the return of growing your own to eat your own, carbon footprints and climate warming, has meant compost has become the main source of fertility for many gardeners. Further problems from landfill, the expense of refuse collection and the general greening of us all has meant composting has almost become an end worthy in itself and not just a means for growing better and healthier plants. Oh well, who cares, as long as we're all doing it anyway.

Left: Piles of any organic wastes reduce to richly mineralised soil if left long enough

What happens in a compost heap?

All things decompose, decay, rot and break down eventually; it's just that some may take a very long time to do so. Composting speeds up the process so that the materials are converted to a brown, friable, soil-like 'compost' in a matter of months, not decades. It is amazing, no matter what bizarre mixture of raw materials go in, once these compost, the result is always similar: a sweet, brown, crumbly, soil-like material that is a good fertiliser, soil improver and mulch that also kills or discourages many pests and prevents diseases in plants grown with it. Compost really is muck and magic!

In an active compost bin the raw materials are first attacked by all sorts of microbes, bacteria and fungi, and gnawed, chewed and swallowed by small creatures such as woodlice, and mostly by worms. In particular, red brandling worms seem especially useful. All these creatures, big and small, take the sugars, celluloses, starches, and so on, converting them into population explosions and a lot of excreta. In this initial phase, in a good compost heap, the mass heats up with all their activity, then other varieties of microbes take over and the breakdown proceeds more quickly and more thoroughly. Populations of each sort of micro-life become a food source for others, and so on. Each birth is soon a death and/or a meal, creating yet more lives and more excreta, which is itself another food resource for yet something else.

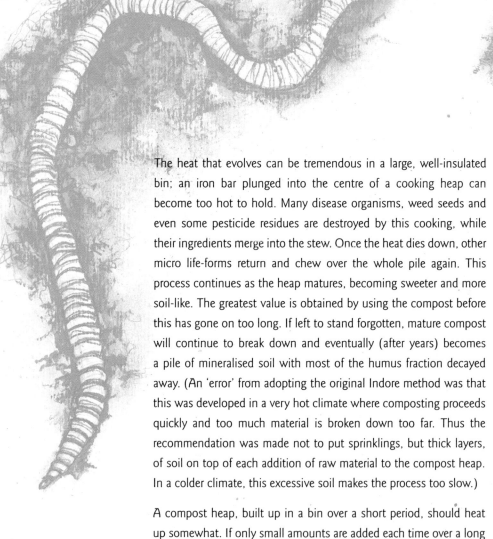

The heat that evolves can be tremendous in a large, well-insulated bin; an iron bar plunged into the centre of a cooking heap can become too hot to hold. Many disease organisms, weed seeds and even some pesticide residues are destroyed by this cooking, while their ingredients merge into the stew. Once the heat dies down, other micro life-forms return and chew over the whole pile again. This process continues as the heap matures, becoming sweeter and more soil-like. The greatest value is obtained by using the compost before this has gone on too long. If left to stand forgotten, mature compost will continue to break down and eventually (after years) becomes a pile of mineralised soil with most of the humus fraction decayed away. (An 'error' from adopting the original Indore method was that this was developed in a very hot climate where composting proceeds quickly and too much material is broken down too far. Thus the recommendation was made not to put sprinklings, but thick layers, of soil on top of each addition of raw material to the compost heap. In a colder climate, this excessive soil makes the process too slow.)

A compost heap, built up in a bin over a short period, should heat up somewhat. If only small amounts are added each time over a long period, little heating will occur. However, if a bin is filled all in one go, or turned and mixed after the initial accumulation, then the heating will be impressive. This 'cooking' time lasts only a couple of weeks. A second turning may be worthwhile to give another 'burn' for another fortnight or so. This also makes for greater uniformity, as ideally the outside is returned to the middle and vice versa, giving all parts a turn cooking in the hotter middle. After a turning and cooking, or even three, the maturing process may be allowed to proceed for a few months or more. The compost should be ready for use within the year, two at the most. For certain crops, such as for potato or runner bean trenches, compost can be taken even sooner whilst rougher. For most purposes, it is better well matured and when it has dried out somewhat and so can be passed through a coarse sieve. This makes a more attractive, more uniform compost. The sieved-out spoil of undecayed detritus, such as bits of bone and woody stems, are returned to the next heap for a second pass where they also act as 'starters', carrying an inoculation of all the right microbes.

After sieving, compost varies slightly by texture, colour and fertility value, mostly according to the raw materials. The pH or acidity balance is made alkaline by the addition of lime or wood ashes, but generally otherwise compost is slightly acidic. Home-made compost is always remarkably similar to expensive loam or peat-based potting compost or dark, rich fertile soil. Indeed, that is pretty much exactly what it is, but one formed in months, not millennia.

Health and Safety

In these litigious days when free will has been stifled by the dead hand of bureaucracy, I must beg your attention for a safety announcement. Compost-making presumably kills even fewer people than flying, but we must obey the nanny state and recognise the greed of lawyers. I must recommend you wear suitable gloves, mask and protective clothing when working with compost. Any cut, prick or damage to your skin should be given medical treatment, especially as rats may have soiled the offending item. I need not remind you to 'wash before eating' and not to add compost to your sandwiches. It would also be sensible to have a tetanus vaccination, first aid box and a fire extinguisher...

What to put on a compost heap

One of the rules to remember is that almost anything that has ever lived can be composted. Only a few items need to be excluded and some others given a bit of pre-treatment. In general, anything that would rot away slowly if left lying around becomes ideal fodder for composting. So that includes old feather pillows, woolly pullovers and cotton socks, as well as the vegetable peelings, food wastes and garden weeds. To help them compost quickly, as mentioned before, dry stuff needs mixing with moist and vice versa. It really is the case of the more the merrier; the more different things that

Left: We all throw away huge amounts of 'tired' food - as well as the peelings and wastes - the environmental cost can be reduced by turning these into fertility and enhanced crops

are mixed together, the better the composting and the fertility produced.

Different raw materials have different minerals and trace elements making up their composition; one is bringing more potash, another more phosphate, a bit of magnesium here, some calcium there. Each weed, leaf, twig, potato peeling or rotten tomato carries tiny amounts of different trace elements, as well as material ripe for composting. Suddenly, weeding a path or bed is not simply tidying or removing the competition to our plants, but it becomes a harvesting of green manures rich in trace elements (see Appendix, page 110). Even pruning and hedge trimming become harvests, especially if tougher bits are chopped up first or aged in a slow bin. A bed of stinging nettles by a ditch is more pleasure to clear three times a year when it's seen as future bags of potting compost. And the ditch dredgings, too, become a valuable additive to the compost cake, bringing microbially-rich muck and finely divided mineral silts to the mixture.

Mix fresh green stuff with old dry stuff.

Collection, pre-treatments and raw material holding

Most people misconstrue filling a compost bin as the same as making compost. Some remember the classic sequencing of layers of this or that being added until the bin is full. Others remember the interleaving sprinkling of soil and/or lime to sweeten the heap. But really, so far is only half the job; this bit is the collection of enough wastes to make a proper compost heap – one that cooks. Once the materials are assembled, the next important part is mixing in order that they can heat up properly. Even so, materials do tend to arrive piecemeal until the bin is full, whether it will receive a turn and mix or not. To prevent the middle getting soggy and the sides ignored, each new addition should be spread evenly across the top of the existing pile and then covered with a sprinkling of earth – or, better, some sievings from a recent batch of good compost and/or lime or wood ashes.

It's quite possible to take each and every item to the bin as it becomes available but, naturally, it makes sense to have a collection system for ingredients such as the kitchen waste. Any container, preferably with a lid, will do, and when placed in the kitchen it can receive the peelings, out of dates and left-on-plate materials, any paper or cardboard packaging, and liquid wastes too. Because no-one wants to go through these to pull out the no-nos (glass, metal, etc.) the container should be well policed. If items such as withered apples or greened potatoes are to be discarded, ideally they should be chopped up before being put in the container. And mouldy yoghurts compost better without their plastic containers! Individual

Right: Pre-soaking newspaper and cardboard in filthy water speeds up their breakdown

batches of peelings, etc. can be collected on sheets of newspaper which are then wrapped and binned. This keeps the bin nicer, sweeter, and also ensures the paper is moistened and mixes into the compost heap well.

Likewise, if you are filling a bucket or wheelbarrow with assorted garden wastes as you work, it makes sense to chop up the twiggy stuff before it becomes intermingled with the weeds, leaves, and so on. And keep the thorny stuff to one side to burn! The smaller the stuff is divided the better, especially where a tough skin is designed to prevent decay, such as with carrots or apples. Twiggy material, in particular, needs to be chopped up as short as possible. Small quantities can be cut with secateurs or chopped with a sharp spade; larger amounts may need a power or hand shredder. These can reduce woody prunings (and fingers) to chips or shreds which then compost easily when mixed with other wastes. In the larger garden, a few well-positioned, lidded, plastic buckets or dustbins make excellent temporary catch-alls that can be emptied after the day's work, or weekly.

These receptacles can also be used to pre-treat pernicious weeds and twiggy or dry material. The Romans noticed how rotting under water killed both the roots of weeds and their seeds – it's as simple as that. It may be foolish to include any pernicious weed root, such as couch grass or bindweed, or any weed in full seed in your compost unless burnt to ash or pre-treated first. So rot risky weeds under water (or in another dirty liquid) for a few weeks and then the whole lot can be added to the bin (see page 63 for the value of grey water). Alternatively, the liquid may be used, well diluted, as a liquid feed and just the slurry and tougher bits added to the compost. No land-weed root, bulb or seed survives weeks of total immersion in a dark container. (The lid not only excludes light, but also keeps the whiff in.) Dry stuff, such as leaves, paper, cardboard and twiggy material, may also benefit

from pre-soaking in water or other dirty liquids. A plastic dustbin makes an excellent holding tank for revolting liquids that can be used to moisten your compost when needed.

Dustbins also make good holding bays in the compost corner for stuff that is awaiting something else to mix with, and for storing the sieved final product. However, plastic bags are cheaper and function just as well, though they are even less visually attractive. Woven plastic bags are good for leaves as they allow air to pass through, but lose too much goodness with wetter wastes.

Left: Small bins make handy collectors for weeds which can be withered and half-dead by the time they're emptied for composting **Above:** Drowning weeds in water kills their roots and their seeds, and makes a vile brew to wet the compost pile or use diluted as a liquid feed

Which composting approach best suits your needs?

Just as there are many variables to making a cake, there are many slight variations to compost making, and there are as many types of compost bin as cake tins. Each has advantages and drawbacks (to be dealt with later), but on the whole these are irrelevant – it's only the container. The original Indore method mentioned earlier includes too much soil, but it is still the template for many of the other approaches I will describe here, such as the slow bin, the rotary bin and the nitre bed. However, almost all methods start with collecting different raw materials which are interleaved and coated with soil or older compost to inoculate them, while held in a retaining container or the final bin.

Right: A pair of easily removable slat-sided wooden, or New Zealand style, bins are a most suitable choice for many gardeners

The main consideration with any method is to match the size of your bin to the amount of material you have to compost. As the compost ideally needs to be turned and mixed, then matured, it really helps to have two or three bins. In the larger garden or allotment, or on the keen scavenger's plot, you usually find at least three compost bins: one for filling, one 'cooking' and maturing, and another being emptied and used. Alongside these may also be a leaf-mould container, a 'slow' bin for woodier stuff or a wildlife pile, and a wormery or snailery, too. Each is a different way of converting various wastes more effectively or pre-treating them before composting.

Composting methods may need to vary somewhat with the season and the region. Compost heaps made during the colder months or regions require more and better mixing and thicker insulation to cook well, while those made in drier warmer seasons and places may need much more water adding to get them to 'cook'. Alternatively, bins filled in wetter times or regions require less water mixing in, as the ingredients are moister already and the bins probably need roofing to stop cold rain arresting the process. Likewise, different mixtures of raw materials require slightly different treatments to work well and quickly, especially where huge amounts of one thing are to be composted, such as grass clippings or horse manure. Generally, dry stuff needs mixing with moist and vice versa.

But the simplest rule is that bigger is better. Bigger heaps are obviously more work to accumulate and turn than smaller ones, but they do compost much more effectively with fewer turns. It is the smaller ones that take more turning – but then at least there is not much stuff to move. Don't worry, though, whatever you do the result will still be compost, it may just take longer to get there.

Forking soil over dry wastes to inoculate the layer, in a quadruple-size bin

Slow bins and faster bins

As I've already mentioned, it all composts anyway, it's just a matter of time. Some people may wish to do the absolute minimum to get rid of annoying wastes, in which case a large bin and just heaving the stuff in will work. But it could smell and attract vermin. Covering each addition with a sprinkling of soil much reduces these risks. Eventually, the bin fills and you start another. If the first is dug out it will usually be found to have rotted down piecemeal unless it has been standing for a very long time. The lack of mixing or pre-treatment means twiggy material, large lumps of anything and dry stuff often come through unaltered within a matrix of well-decayed material. The uncomposted bits need to be removed and added to the next compost heap – preferably chopped up and wetted first.

To prevent such patchy composting it really does make sense to chop or cut all the twiggy, bushy and tougher material that is slow to rot, such as Brussels sprouts stalks, before adding them to the heap in the first place. However, a straightforward alternative to such pre-treatment is to run a parallel slow heap. This is simply another container or bin, preferably with an open top that allows rain to wet the contents. The tougher, rougher material is not put in the usual compost bin but in this one, leaving the other to compost materials quicker so that they break down more evenly. Every other year or so the contents of a slow bin can be disgorged, the toughest remnants returned, and any broken-down material added to the next compost bin.

Right: The sides may be falling to bits, but you can ensure good insulation and real waterproofing for the top, and the contents will soon compost, mature and dry out ready for sieving

A wildlife pile is similar. Resembling an unlit bonfire (and it is in real danger of becoming lit if placed too near a fence or footpath), this pile of stalks and sticks, bushy prunings and even thorny waste is allowed to accumulate for years. Then, one day, it's broken down with the top tough stuff used to start another pile. Underneath the bottom of the old pile is some lovely dark, peaty material, like dirty sawdust, to mix into the next compost heap.

All this withstanding, a faster bin is our more usual wish, and there are many ways to achieve it. As already mentioned, mixing a lot of different ingredients creates a faster breakdown in the first place. Turning and remixing the ingredients makes the process work more quickly and more evenly. Reducing the size of the materials by pre-chopping or shredding improves it more. As I will deal with further on, we can also add activators or rapidly decomposing manures as yet another way to speed up the process. Simply getting more material and making the heap bigger also works very well, as it retains more heat; and for the same reason adding insulation can help speed up the rot. Small bins lose heat as fast as it's created; wrapping them in layers of insulation stops the heat loss and helps the ingredients cook. The problem with adding insulation to retain heat is that this then excludes air, the value of which we will come to in a bit. However, most heat is lost upwards, thus the sides can be left partially exposed to allow air ingress while an insulating cover on top will retain a large proportion of the heat. This cover ought to lay flat on the heap and a separate lid or roof should be provided to throw off, or throw in, rain. You need not insulate the base, as it would have minimal effect anyway because heat rises and it could prevent wildlife passing up and down. In particular, worms do much of the processing but need to leave when the pile heats and return as it cools.

Right: Twiggy stuff is slow to compost, so can be piled in a dry shady corner as a wildlife refuge

The advantages of aeration and turning techniques

As mentioned, a compost heap needs to breathe. Although some processes can take place that are anaerobic (need no oxygen), those better, and less smelly, ones (the majority) need oxygen. Now keeping the sides relatively open, or at least perforated, and only the top insulated allows some air in for as long as the heap stands. Some experimenters have built bins with underground venting using pipes and air-bricks to allow air to enter from below, but this does not create much better aeration and risks isolating the contents from the soil beneath.

In practice, the most effective way of getting better aeration immediately is to mix or remix the contents, with all the other benefits this brings. The materials that have most problems are wet claggy ones prone to packing down. Mixing these with drier coarser material, such as straw, sawdust or shredded paper, usually helps by allowing more air to pass through, and oxygen is also added during the mixing when the claggy materials are loosened. Thus, the value of turning a heap comes from both the mixing and aeration.

Now the aim is to remove the contents of a bin, breaking them up and mixing them as you go, ideally simultaneously placing the old outside as the new middle and the old middle as the new outside. At the same time, you should check for moistness and correct it as the material is repacked. This is where having two or more bins is handy, as the contents can be moved from one to the other in one neat go. The alternative is double handling, where the lot is put out temporarily onto a sheet of plastic and then reloaded with any corrective added.

Now it is possible to just accumulate materials in a bin and never mix them – with bigger bins this is especially so – but the result will be relatively slow coming. The digging out of the contents and the mixing or remixing really does make for an impressive improvement in quality and speed, and as turning is most needed with the smaller bins (because these lose heat the fastest), it is fortunate and convenient they do not contain much material to evict, mess about with and replace.

Think about it: what would a cake be like if the ingredients were just put in the cake tin and cooked? Mixing makes the cake much, much better! So go mix your bin, and then do it again a month later and make the very best compost 'cake'.

Limed if needed, this is now inoculated with soil and, ideally, previously successful compost

Rotary, self-mixing and stirring bins

A rotary composter can work well in the right situation

There are several versions of these. Some enable the container to be revolved horizontally, mixing the contents as they rotate, others employ a paddle or screw system to mix the contents. These are all grand ideas: more mixing equals better compost. However, in practice I find these less than ideal; perhaps they may work better in warmer climes or where the main bulk is leaves and dryish grass clippings, or material such as strawy pony or goat manure. The smaller-sized bins of any type suffer from the common problem of insufficient size and insulation, and even given fantastic ingredients and vigorous agitation could never heat up. If a bin is big enough to heat well, the frail human body makes a poor job of stirring any paddle or screw in it well enough to make a difference. Those where the whole bin rotates, like a huge front-loading washing machine or concrete mixer, can work a bit better, as with these the materials may occasionally be agitated sufficiently. However, there's a tendency to pack them into a claggy mass which resists agitation and is hard to break up or dig out later. These are also not inexpensive items; going for more insulation and manual remixing is fundamentally more effective and far cheaper.

Anaerobic digesters, nitre beds and middens

What we are after with composting is to produce a good compost; one that is sweet to smell and pleasant to handle, free of detritus and full of fertility, much like rich soil. However, you just might want to compost for other purposes, too.

As I've explained, the composting process gives off heat and some people have warmed entire houses with huge compost heaps by extracting this heat using embedded flexible water pipes. Making a compost heap in your greenhouse may make it a bit warmer but it will take up a lot of space and the heat is not produced rapidly enough to beat a frosty night. However, it makes sense to position a hot bed there anyway (see page 86). It would not be difficult to pack large drums with well-mixed material, to roll these under the benches as they start to cook, and out again when they've cooled for repacking. But even so, they would only provide background heat and never enough to defeat an unusually cold night.

There is another slight problem with using a compost process under cover. Although a compost heap or bin need not smell (because the topmost layer of soil and/or lime cleans the escaping gases), if you put one in a greenhouse, or anywhere else, with or without a cover, or use a high proportion of any sort of manure, it may pong a bit. Only some of those gases are useful to plants – carbon dioxide is, but the smelly ones, especially the ammoniacal, nitrogenous or sulphurous gases, are bad for plants.

Anaerobic composting (ie composting without air at all) makes many smelly compounds; thus waste rotted in a plastic bag stinks far more than if rotted with access to air. While the gases are sealed in the bag they multiply the populations of microflora that are tolerant of them and kill others. This may be of use when destroying weed seeds or roots or eliminating some pests or disease pathogens, however, the process does stink, makes materials unpleasant to handle or have around, and does not break down woody materials very well. It is, however, expedient that if wastes cannot be added to a bin straight away then they should be in almost completely sealed bags or bins. By excluding air they will only be able to rot anaerobically, and thus more slowly, and so can await proper composting without, hopefully, losing too much fertility.

You see, all that whiffy gaseous stuff, if combined with lime or soil, makes fertiliser. That is why lime, wood ashes, soil or expired compost (already used as a potting compost and returned for re-invigorating) are added to every layer and used as a thick topping for finishing off the ideal heap. It's a bit like a gas mask filtering out the nasties.

Anaerobic digesters as such, are another method of composting but are rather beyond the scope of this book. Rot down compostable wastes in water with agitation and you produce methane, lots of it, and of course those nasty smells which need cleaning out. However, the methane can be burnt for warmth, and the slurry left over does have fertility value. I can envisage a greenhouse heater powered this way with the gas made all day, stored until needed at night, then burnt in a conventional heater. (Be warned, though, this is dangerous and explosive technology that's really not for the home experimenter.)

Another arcane art is the nitre bed. This was a way to make a very nitrogenous mix as rich as seagull guano. As noted above; soil, and especially chalk, combine with those whiffy gases given off by some of the composting processes to make natural fertilisers, such as calcium nitrate. Thus, if you make a very rich, very chalky, well-aerated compost heap and mix it frequently, continuously wetting it with urine, you get an incredibly strong fertiliser of even richer material than you started with, formed by the proliferation of nitrifying bacteria fixing nitrogen from the air. This enriched weapons-grade compost can then be mixed, much as with worm compost, with poorer composts to improve them for potting or other purposes.

A kitchen midden or waste pile is just that: all wastes, whatever they are, simply dumped somewhere. I trust that by reading this book you will not be making one, however, you may discover one if you acquire a new home. A midden will probably be covered with stinging nettles or, if ancient, elderberry trees, as these love such a rich site. The materials, though not totally decayed, may well still be a very good source of fertility. The woody bits can

go into a slow heap and the soft trash can be mixed into a proper compost heap. If in quantity, old stuff from a midden can be recomposted in bulk and activated using fresh grass clippings and urine or lime or chalk (unless the compost is needed for acid lovers). A huge heap of semi-decayed grass clippings, leaves or stable manure can be treated similarly and mined out and recomposted properly before being applied to the soil. Woodpiles left too long also decay down, leaving a sawdust-like material that needs recomposting to utilise the locked up fertility.

Above left: A sprinkling of lime absorbs gases and makes a sweeter (more alkaline) compost
Above right: Mixing dead leaves with fresh grass clippings overcomes drawbacks of both

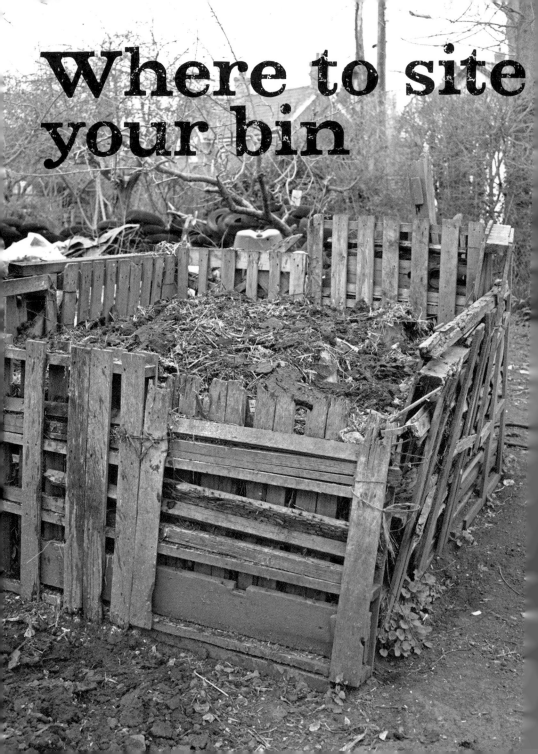

Where to site your bin

Where you site your bin makes a difference. In a cold place it will be slow, in a hot corner, quicker. If you put it somewhere windy it will dry out more. In a large garden it's foolish to put it at the top of a slope, as you will push many barrowloads of material there and bring few back. If you neglect the lime or soil coatings or have a lot of nitrogenous materials, it may pong, and if it is without a lid it will attract flies or, worse, vermin. Thus, it's generally not a good idea to site a compost bin near open windows or patios. If you position it in an inconvenient corner, stuff may be difficult to take there; an open area that can be used for mixing is handy, so putting it by a lawn or drive (using a protective plastic sheet) is more convenient. It is said that elder trees and birch make good companions for compost areas, whilst pines and other evergreens are poor ones. This is likely as most waxy evergreen leaves have compounds in them that prevent seeds germinating and alter soil microflora. Indeed, if small twigs of birch and the soft green stems and leaves of elderberry are added to a bin they decay quite quickly, whilst any quantity of the evergreen or conifer leaves may come through almost untouched.

When siting your bin you also ought to be sure it cannot potentially leach into a watercourse, or, of course, cause offence to anyone. Although there are countless sensible reasons for positioning a compost heap in a chicken run this is now banned in the UK because of possible cross contamination with meat products from the kitchen...

Although it may be useful to have solid foundations for the corners or sides of a bin, it is not a good idea to place it on concrete or any other solid surface. The worms and so on cannot go up and down freely, but worse the liquids leaching out will be a problem. These could be caught in a tray and used, diluted, as a liquid feed or simply returned to the compost to moisten the bin.

Left: A quadruple size bin with all internal slats the best way, vertical, so compost slips down easily

What to use when making a compost bin

The best materials to use when making bins are recycled plastics, as these ought to last. Small bins can only be sensibly made of plastic, preferably double walled, however, wood is commonly used for convenience. Old wooden pallets tied at the corners or broken down and remade as smaller units do not last more than a few years, but they are usually free and easily replaceable. Do not use creosote (now banned) or other wood preservers as these can halt the composting process. Old cooking oil is a relatively harmless treatment or charring the wood ensures greater longevity. Bricks, blocks, railway sleepers and so on make good sides and backs, but at least the front ought to be easily removable for emptying. Solid concrete, brickwork, slabs of plywood or other totally impermeable walls are not suitable, though with more mixing or when used on a grand scale they could work fairly well.

Right: All-plastic bins should last well - though I'd drill ventilation holes in at least the bottom slats.

Insulation is an important point but, as previously noted, it should not prevent air circulation through the sides. Smaller bins need insulating in order to work well and the small amount of material inside can be easily re-mixed to give sufficient aeration to cook. Bubble plastic wrapped around them is probably the best but layers of materials such as dry newspaper or cardboard will retain heat. Cardboard is handy for slipping inside pallets and, once it breaks down, it can be added to the next bin. Insulation is needed most after turning and mixing as, in many heaps, insufficient breakdown takes place until then and so the materials simply accumulate. In winter, additional insulation is important as the heat is more rapidly lost and the outside of a heap or bin may stay too cool to compost well.

The top of the bin loses most heat so this needs the most insulation. A plastic sheet should be put on top of the contents first to stop the damp materials wetting the insulation, which is placed on top of the plastic. The insulation can be old carpet, old clothes, cardboard, bubble plastic, or balls of newspaper simply stuffed into plastic bags, but it all needs to be arranged for quick removal and replacement. Ideally, it should sit inside the bin, on top of the contents, with another plastic sheet or a proper roof above it to keep the rain off. Although sometimes letting the rain in might be an advantage, generally it will just be too much wet, and too cold, to suit composting.

Camouflage is a moot point when it comes to compost bins. I do not consider a neat bin in a tidy area unsightly – but it's hardly a decorative feature. It could be, though; there are designs for compost heaps after the manner of beehives, dog kennels and even wells, but most of these sacrifice practicality. Yet there is potential; the appearance could be a façade with the real bin within – accessibility is the key here. Otherwise, if space allows, site the bin within a designated utilitarian area, surround it with fences or hedges or a pergola all covered with climbers and it's gone. Such an area is also handy as somewhere to stack materials awaiting inclusion, bags of finished sieved compost awaiting use, and stores of similar materials such as leaf-mould, sand and rotted-down turf loam.

A: 'EASY' WAY. AS PALLETS COME, BOTH SLATS SAME WAY

B: RIGHT WAY. INSIDE SLATS VERTICAL—OUTSIDE HORIZONTAL

C: STEP-BY-STEP CONTENTS — BOTTOM LAYER OF PAPER AND CARDBOARD. THEN ADD WASTES, WATER AND SPRINKLE SOIL OR ASHES. REPEAT.

A

B

C

LIFT-OFF LID AND WATER-PROOF COVER

PLASTIC SHEET

DOUBLE-WALLED WOODEN PALLET SIDES WITH GAPS

BRICK BASE (OPTIONAL)

The perfect compost bin

STUFFED WITH NEWSPAPER BALLS AND/OR CARDBOARD

What will compost and what will not?

Anything that has ever lived will compost, but the highly processed, such as leather, and the tough, such as big bones and wood, take a long time unless they are pre-processed, but plastic, stone, brick, tile, glass and metal never rot. It helps to keep different stuff separated out from the start. Sorting these out later when sieving the finished product is more time-consuming than extracting them from the fresh wastes beforehand. And, as suggested on page 32, it may help to have a slow bin and a fast bin for slow- and quick-rotting materials if the tougher ones cannot be chopped or shredded first.

Left: Wood ashes are an excellent addition and keep a bin sweet, as does lime

Common raw materials

Here are some of the more common raw materials that can be added to a compost bin, along with a few suggestions as to pre-processing and alternative uses.

Garden wastes

Use everything; all the windfall and reject fruits, fresh leaves and dead ones, light shrubby trimmings and most green prunings, the lawn and path edgings and weeds from paths, the dead headings, trimmed vegetable leaves and roots. The unwanted surpluses, once they wither and before they rot, the gunge from gutters, water butts, ditches and the bottom of the pool – all make good compost. The greater the variety of source materials the better, and the range of elements accumulated by different weeds is inestimable. Indeed, weeding becomes gathering free mineral resources (see Appendix, page 110). If you live by the shore, seaweed is the best material of all to add. Next comes stinging nettles, grown almost anywhere; these give several cuts or pullings a year and rot down to a rich, dark, peat-like quality and cook well when included in quantity.

'All that has ever lived will compost to feed the soil, making even more crops and wastes to compost in turn.'

However, some materials have other uses, too. First, twiggy stuff can be pea sticks or props for straggling ornamentals – they'll still come to the bin once they are old, worn and dirty. Any hollow-stemmed or stalky material makes wildlife shelters once cut and tied in neat bundles – sweet corn stems are especially good for ladybirds. Bundles hidden away in evergreens and dense hedges help many tiny critters overwinter and provide summer nests for useful types of wasp and bee. Seed heads can be collected up, dried, and saved to feed the birds in winter. Leaves of borage and comfrey may be rotted down to make a liquid feed. Surplus and waste potatoes, turnips and carrots halved and hollowed out make demon slug traps, and then they can be added to the bin with the slugs cut in half, squashed, or whatever. These too will compost, adding back a little fertility to repay for all that which they have eaten.

Household wastes – kitchen

(Note: local by-laws and national legislation may forbid the inclusion of certain items. If in doubt, check with a legal advisor or risk becoming a composting criminal.)

In practice, any and all food items, cooked or otherwise, can be composted, though it's better if any larger chunks or portions are broken up. Don't forget to break the skin of discarded roots, such as potatoes and carrots and chop wizened fruits. Liquid wastes, such as 'the vegetable boiling water', coffee and tea dregs, etc., can be collected separately or in the same container where they can help soak drier materials. Wine and beer dregs and fermenting liquids are especially useful as they're full of micro-organisms already.

Orange and citrus skins make grand slug traps first and can be composted after.

Bread, biscuits and cakes that are merely stale could be frozen or dried, or mixed with fats, dried fruits, seeds, etc., to feed birds in winter. (You get repaid with pest control and gain fertility from their droppings and feathers, and a pretty song.)

Right: Don't compost seed heads before saving the seed to feed the birds in winter

Anything other than small amounts of oil, fat, cheese or meat may be better given to a friend with a dog rather than included in the more modest compost bin. These are slow to rot and may attract vermin. However, in bigger bins, if divided up amongst loads of other stuff and mixed in well, they will compost, adding valuable nutrients.

Non-food wastes, such as paper towels, paper bags, egg cartons and cardboard packaging, and so on, compost, especially if soaked first, as will tea bags and coffee filter papers. Waxed, aluminised and plastic-coated card is better excluded.

Eggshells are mostly calcium, so really large quantities should not be added to small compost bins intended for ericaceous lime-hating plants, though the odd few in larger bins are unlikely to cause problems.

Bones are important; they contain phosphorus combined with lime, which is valuable for promoting root growth, so they're worth making special efforts to compost rather than dump. Cooked bones should not be given to pets as they splinter and can hurt or kill, and likewise they're much slower to break down when composted than raw green bones. If your compost is sieved before use, any surviving bones can be picked out and transferred to the next bin, where they will soften and break up, making their phosphates available. Large, heavy bones compost more slowly than small ones and pass through several bins. Such bones can be baked or burnt on the remains of a barbecue or bonfire, their ash recovered and added to the bin – though not in great quantity for composts intended for ericaceous plants, as the ash will be quite alkaline. Big bones can easily be pounded to bits once burnt as they become quite brittle. Teeth may survive several successive compost bins, even after burning – and those with metal fillings or crowns would be a bit of a dead giveaway. Oops!

Left: The worms for composting kitchen wastes are smallish red ones, up to say a small finger length

Household wastes
— other

The contents of the vacuum cleaner bag are worth investigating carefully before adding to a bin, so tip them onto a sheet of newspaper first. They are usually mostly lint, hair and fluff, and human skin cells, which will compost rapidly but need wetting or mixing with damper material first. Some bizarrely consider road dust tramped onto the carpet too dangerous to transfer to the compost – best not go outdoors at all then...

Packaging cardboards and newspaper rot well if soaked in nasty liquids and if they are not added in thick layers – corrugated cardboard is especially loved by the red brandlings that work in wormeries. Waxed or plastic-coated cardboard, heavily glossed paper, glittery, silvery, mock-gold Christmas wrapping and magazines are probably best excluded as these contain undesirable materials.

Do not forget the toilet roll middles, dead flowers, shredded documents, worn-out cotton or woollen clothes and socks, woolly blankets, fur and feather items, feather pillows, and even your old silk scarf. All need well soaking in vile liquids then interleaving with more active material, such as grass clippings or nettles, but compost they will – even quicker if they are cut into smaller bits first.

Old carpets (preferably cotton or wool, not rubber- or latex-backed and not moth-proofed) will compost but may make good floor, wall, or even ceiling coverings in draughty garden sheds first, or they can be used as temporary paths or weed-excluding mulches. But once they do start to rot they can be well soaked and added in. Coir mats are remarkably slow to compost but will go eventually.

Then there are the human wastes. Finger- and toenail clippings and hair are slow-release sources of nitrogen, so include them. Your urine is also a

rich source of fertility (see page 65), however, for now I draw the line there. Although composting toilets are quite practical their time has not yet come.

Above: The dry shredded paper with soggy rotten apples it cushioned makes a good composting layer

Awkward items

Those awkward problematical items of weeds in seed and the roots of pernicious weeds can be killed simply by immersing them in a butt of water or other vile liquid for a few weeks before adding them to the compost. Utilised by the Romans but apparently forgotten, this works really well.

Really thorny stuff is, for safety, best burnt and the ashes added, or instead the thorny stems can be cut to uniform lengths and tied in bundles rolled around with newspaper or cardboard for use as more wildlife shelters, as with hollow-stemmed stuff.

Actual diseased material is a moot point, though. I believe it is okay when included in big cooking bins, but it may be more problematical in smaller ones that do not heat up. It seems obvious that most diseases are already present in the garden if they're on the wastes. However, in a compost heap they can be attacked by the plethora of micro-life who can consume the disease organisms to become a hungry population of new predators seeking the next batch when returned to the soil. (But see Problems, on page 68).

Evergreen leaves give off phytotoxic chemicals which slow the pace of composting and, although adding a few may not hurt, a larger quantity should never be included unless pre-processed. Ideally this should be done by shredding and storing them for a year or three while mixed with grass clippings or vile liquids or lime.

Grass clippings are a mixed blessing; they are excellent when mixed intimately with dry and cellulose-rich materials, but they can be a problem in quantity as they pack down, excluding air and making an anaerobic mass that persists for a long time. They're also much more valuable used as mulches around trees, shrubs, roses, soft fruit and larger vegetables. Laid as a mulch in thin layers, clippings do not make a nasty sludge but a fibrous mat which suppresses weeds. (If weeds break through, dump another layer on them.)

'Thorny stems can be cut to uniform lengths and tied in bundles rolled around with newspaper or cardboard for use as wildlife shelters, as with hollow-stemmed stuff.'

Activators

A well-mixed heap or bin of diverse materials, well moistened, rarely needs an activator. Using a sprinkling of old compost, earth or sievings from another heap introduces all the right sorts of organisms, and often incorporating stinging nettles or grass clippings is quite sufficient to get a bin cooking. Any sort of manure usefully increases the nitrogen to carbon ratio, while also adding all sorts of micro-organisms and increasing the rate of breakdown more rapidly. In order of the increased composting activity they produce, I rate the value of manures as follows: bird droppings (chicken or pigeon is best), cow (from breeding stock, then fattening and milking stock), as the first four-legged choice, then horse, followed by sheep, goat, rabbit, guinea pig, llama and alpaca. Pig manure is cold and slow but rich; goose and duck droppings are wet and need mixing with dry stuff; cat and dog dung is unpleasant and poses health issues so it is probably best buried by a tree. Sadly, composting human dung currently puts you in the 'too eccentric to be a nice neighbour' camp.

Adding lime keeps compost sweet, as mentioned earlier, but it also increases the rate of breakdown. Raw or quick lime is far too dangerous, we use common chalk or limestone, preferably really finely ground. Dolomitic limestone is considered better, as it also contains magnesium. Calcified seaweed lime is best, as it also introduces many trace elements and the porous texture invites microbes to settle and proliferate. A compost made with plenty of lime is particularly well composed for vegetables and stone fruits, but it is not good for ericaceous, acid-loving plants.

Wood ashes have a spread of trace elements, though mainly potassium. Those made from smaller twigs and stems have higher levels than those from log woods; they are also quite alkaline and so, as with lime, should not be included in compost bound for ericaceous subjects. Mixing lime and wood ashes with soil for a topmost layer makes any bin smell sweeter, as this will absorb smelly gases.

Soot from fires burning only clean fuels and with no plastic, etc., is peculiar stuff. It could have small amounts of nasty chemicals while the black, finely divided carbon is good for darkening soils, making them warmer. It is probably best excluded nowadays, though I use mine to make a feed for pineapples and citrus.

Left: Amost all manures are excellent activators

My chickens poo whilst roosting onto wood shavings to make weapons-grade compost activator

Commercial compost activators are often just expensive forms of nitrogen-rich chemical fertilisers, while a gallon or two of urine is as good and cheaper. However, these probably do little harm and everyone needs a living. If you have a sack of conventional chemical fertiliser, one way of using it up with less harm to the soil life is to put it through a compost heap – either sprinkled on moist, very high-carbon materials such as sawdust, paper or cardboard, or diluted down and watered on as with other dirty waters. A sprinkling of blood, fish and bone meal, or just fishmeal, is an expensive but effective activator. Alfalfa meal is said to be good, but it is not widely available.

Herbal activators, such as those recommended by Maye E. Bruce in her Quick Return compost-making method (basically the same as we are using) are an interesting concept and rely on the idea that certain herbs stimulate the best micro-life to process the compost more quickly and/or more thoroughly. Very similar are the Bio-dynamic preparations originally conceived by Rudolf Steiner; the founder of Bio-dynamics was asked by farmers how to improve their impoverished soils and suggested adding compost stimulated by his unique preparations. In practice, though, none of these activators have proved necessary but they can do little harm, so why not? And, nothing beats adding a barrowload of manure, a few gallons of urine or a heap of fresh stinging nettles.

The value of water, grey water, sludge, beer dregs and liquid manure

Without sufficient moisture the composting process goes very slowly or arrests entirely. A slight lack of moisture and Fire-fang fungus may proliferate, showing as a white coating over the contents. Excess wet also makes the process slow and promotes anaerobic breakdown and nasty smells – this may happen if too thick layers of wet green weeds, grass clippings or wet manure are added.

To compost well, material needs to be about as moist as a squeezed sponge, and ensuring dry material is wetted before adding helps. It's probably safest to add small amounts of liquids as the bin is filled, otherwise they may run through, but applications can be heavier the deeper the bed of materials. Normally, a top cover and a roof are needed to keep in heat and exclude rain, but these can be removed to allow rain in to dry bins. Using a hose or sprinkler may be easy but it's colder than butt water.

Wetting water need not be clean tap water, indeed, the dirtier the better – not only for nutrients but for even more variety of micro-organisms. So the dregs from the water butt, dirty ditch or pond water with black sludge from the bottom, the drippings from a wormery, your un-drunk beverages (especially beer and wine dregs), soured milk and yoghurt, all these are rich sources of micro-life and boost your heap. They can be watered over each layer as they become available or accumulated in a container, such as a plastic dustbin with a lid, and in which dry stuff such as paper and cardboard can be soaked before being added to the bin.

Your most valuable source of free fertility is your urine. Now, if you are offended by this direction, fine, stop here. However, adding your urine to a bin has distinct benefits. First, it saves sending it down the toilet and wasting clean tap water flushing it away to pollute the rivers and seas. Second, it really is one of the best activators and nutrient sources for your compost, being rich in nitrogen, potassium and animal hormones. Urine, when fresh, is sterile and rarely carries any diseases (excepting apparently some forms of hepatitis); applied fresh it causes no smell, especially if lime, ashes and/or soil are sprinkled on after. Urine can also be accumulated and applied after fermenting, which is how the 'old boys' preferred it. Urine is one of the best dirty waters for pre-soaking materials such as paper and cardboard, as its high nitrogen content balances their high carbon one. It's probably best to refrain from using your urine if you're taking antibiotics or any other life-suppressing substances. Some believe birth-control pill residues in urine may be detrimental to other life forms. Alcohol can be allowed for pragmatic reasons.

Left: It would not be so good if it
were not so disgusting - nothing
human though, honest

Getting more materials

Bigger is always better; small bins process slowly, big ones quickly. Thus, it makes sense to get a bigger bin than you need and to scavenge for more materials to fill it. Neighbours may be happy to give you sacks of grass clippings, weeds and autumn leaves, but their prunings may be more than you want to handle. (Be careful and find out if herbicides have been applied to their grass, as it may arrest the composting or damage plants later.) You may even offer to process their household wastes, though their occasional thoughtless discard may cause embarrassment. Cleaning up old folks' gardens for them can be an act of charity amply rewarded with barrow loads of weeds, lawn edgings and so on, and maybe a friendly chat, tea and cake as well. Tidying up the verge outside and the odd corner of waste ground may seem a good idea but it might tread on toes! Likewise, local businesses may be glad to dispose of waste fruit and vegetables, dead flowers, tea bags, hair trimmings, shredded paper and so on. However, you may come into conflict with the law if you are not careful because you are not a qualified waste-disposal company – check with your local authority what you can and can't do. Collecting seaweed from the shore is probably legally depriving the monarch of their bounty but it seems to be allowed by long practice. And do not forget pondweed – either duck or blanket – which is lovely stuff to add to a bin.

Pondweed can be wound up
on a cane and makes a valuable
compost material

What can go wrong?

Problems, compost concerns and correctives

Sometimes a bin does not heat up and, when broken open, some or all of the contents remain relatively unchanged. Given time, they would undoubtedly decay, but we are necessarily impatient. The answer is usually to fork out the materials onto a plastic sheet, breaking them up into smaller pieces as you go. If they are dry, wet them; if wet, add dry stuff. Then sprinkle on activators and/or fresh green material and pack it all back in the bin again. Ninety-nine times out of a hundred the pile will heat up, cook and compost. Just possibly it may still fail, but only if lots of something really hostile was included, say, too many evergreen leaves or wet manure soaked with disinfectant, or similar.

Right: Really dry stuff can be well placed at the start of a new fill to soak up any liquids draining down

If too wet:

As said previously, remix the material, adding shredded paper, cardboard, straw, hay, leaves, sawdust or other dryish stuff. Too-wet conditions will also probably have leached out nitrogen, so add some of the manures or activators listed previously, or a nitrogenous fertiliser. Be careful to mix thoroughly and do not pack down but leave contents as loosely aerated as possible. Add plenty of lime and/or soil to the topmost layers to absorb ammonia and the gases that wet bins produce.

If too dry:

Again, remix and while the contents are spread out on a plastic sheet, wet them down with dirty water. Add a drop or two of washing-up liquid to better wet really dry stuff. Pack the moistened materials firmly back in the bin and rewet again as you go, if necessary. A bit more nitrogenous waste will again help.

If too acid:

This is often associated with too wet. Usually, in the absence of lime or wood ashes, the materials may rot but remain recognisable, and probably whiff a bit. Remix them, incorporating some lime, wood ashes and/or soil, and to promote heating mix in copious fresh green materials and/or manure. Remember, this compost cannot then be used on ericaceous lime haters.

If too alkaline:

An unlikely eventuality, as most compost becomes slightly acidic. However, if you accidentally included too much lime or wood ashes (or monumental quantities of marble chips, eggshells, snail shells or bone ashes) the best corrective would be to remix with huge quantities of grass clippings and leaves.

If you are scared and concerned about adding material contaminated with diseases or pathogens, be not alarmed. Composting in a bin that heats up kills most disease organisms. (Remember that in compost there are a multiplicity of organisms preying on each other in some way; pest and disease eggs, spores and whatever are all potential food.) Anyway, few new problems can arise from compost made from materials added back to the garden from which they came. It's remotely possible that some disease could be brought in on materials from another garden, and slightly more possibly on kitchen wastes. Even so, I've not found this common, though to be fair it may be happening without our noticing it. So if you are concerned that pernicious and debilitating diseases may possibly be carried by some material, say, the dreaded white rot on onion peelings, either exclude such wastes, burn or bake the life out of them beforehand, or simply make a separate bin for them. The material from that 'suspicious' bin can still be used for a soil enricher, say, when planting a hedge or whatever.

Although a few ornamentals are related to some vegetables, most are not, and vice versa. Thus few of the countless pests and diseases are common to both and their composts can be even more safely exchanged than used on themselves. So compost made from vegetable area and kitchen wastes might be better used in the ornamental area and vice versa.

Doubling up and swapping over like this is a sensible idea anyway in the larger garden or where much extra material is brought in. Pairs of bins are filled, one with mostly vegetable and kitchen wastes and one with other wastes, such as grass clippings, leaves, hedge trimmings, nettles and herbage, etc. The vegetable waste bin is used in the ornamental area or under fruit trees and soft fruit, while the second, less closely related compost, is used for the vegetable beds and can also be made especially richer and better suited with more lime and bone wastes.

Vermin are not a compost problem; rats and mice are an urban problem – they're there anyway, seeing their activity near a compost bin merely indicates their persistent presence. Excluding cheese, meats and so on does not effectively discourage them, as they're still attracted to the warmth and moisture of a bin. It's possible to make a bin vermin-proof with materials such

Right: Only half an apple is consumed - the rest can become food for your vegetables, and don't worry about diseases or residues on the peel, the composting process will break most of them down

as galvanised chicken wire, but more effective is to poison and/or trap them, reducing their numbers before they damage your bin, house or health.

Flies, large and small, can be prevented by covering every addition with grass clippings, ashes, lime or soil. (Adding road kill and other corpses that have been exposed in the open may result in a flush of flies emerging.) Myriads of tiny little flies, like thunder-flies, are a sign of acid, wet conditions, so the compost possibly needs a dressing of soil or lime on top and/or a remixing.

Nasty smells are also invariably a sign of insufficient lime and/or wet conditions and can be easily remedied by remixing with appropriate additives. A good compost bin should smell mushroomy and earthy, not offensive; only when first cooking might it have a richer, more ammoniacal smell and that, again, indicates not enough soil and lime on top. Matured compost definitely should smell sweet of earth, mushrooms and woods.

Flies should not be a problem, but if they occur, are easily remedied with dressings of lime and soil

Which composters for which purpose?

Having different compost bins, especially of various sizes, is useful as not all materials are best handled with just one bin. Obviously, for those with no or only a tiny garden the smallest bin may prove too big, in which case a wormery or pit may be a better solution (see pages 87-91). For small gardens and small households, a council plastic dalek, or preferably two, can be made to work. For the bigger household, bigger garden or keen composter with access to some extra materials, bins of four wooden pallets tied at the corners are simple, cheap and of near optimum size. With copious supplies of materials, more bins, rather than bigger bins may be a better solution, as each is a manageable unit, while really big bins could take too much labour to fill and turn. Generally, though, aim for a slightly bigger bin, get it full by scrounging materials, mix and mature it and there will not often be a problem using up the lovely stuff you'll make.

The smaller or 'council dalek' and other lift offs

As sold or given by councils, these are rarely larger than a plastic dustbin and often much smaller so they compost rather poorly. It's because they're small, insufficiently aerated or insulated and seldom mixed that causes slow composting and rotting, smells and disillusionment. However, for the smaller household and garden with few wastes, these can be made to work. Place them on soil, as they're usually bottomless, then fill them through the top, replacing the lid to keep out problems.

As these daleks are often operated by semi-reluctant owners, the material is also frequently not well chopped or mixed, inappropriate items get included and the sprinklings of soil and/or lime forgotten. Their construction makes a dalek a good container in which to accumulate materials, but not an ideal one in which to compost. The walls are usually impermeable, the lid may seal and the bin sits on the ground so no air can pass through it. Thus you get anaerobic breakdown with attendant problems. Anyway, air can be mixed in so once one is full, lift it off, place it suitably nearby and refill with the accumulated pile. Break this up and mix in fresh green stuff, wet or dry stuff and/or dirty water as you go – do not pack the materials down as air must mix in – then wrap the bin in layers of insulation. It should start to cook after a few days to a week. If not, mix again, adding more activating material, such as manure. Another remix after two or three weeks' time will rekindle the composting process as it starts to fade and finish the job.

As most dalek bins are near airtight, after another month or so, lift away the bin but fashion a lid of some sort to amply cover the exposed pile of materials. This can be as simple as a board on top, an old carpet or plastic sheet. The idea is to keep the rain off and to expose the sides of the pile (so a loose plastic sheet will do) sufficiently to allow air to penetrate and excess moisture to evaporate slowly away. Then the pile can mature for a few months, as oxygen-

breathing creatures such as brandling worms thoroughly rework the materials. You really need two dalek bins: one to fill and one that's cooking/maturing. Have a bucket and scoop of sieved soil or spent compost with added ground lime or chalk already mixed in standing by your dalek, then it will be easy to add a sprinkling to each layer to ensure freedom from flies, smells and so on.

Above: Not ideal but common, the dalek type, is a tad small, not quite well enough insulated, far too airtight, and any idea of removing the finished product through the wee, propped shut, cat flap - ludicrous

Bigger, better bins and slatted sides

These are the better size for most medium and larger gardens and where extra materials are brought in. There are an amazing number of ready-made ones available, but, as previously mentioned, little beats four recycled wooden pallets tied together at the corners. Beware commercial fantasies – vertically slatted sides of flimsy plastic that sort of push up in wobbly bins are tedious and often not fit for purpose. Then, although more rigid vertical slatted sides could work, the idea of extracting matured compost through the exposed hole at the bottom is still impractical. Thus, larger bins made with corner posts and removable horizontal slats, such as the New Zealand bin, make more sense. More slats can be added as the contents rise, and a whole side can be removed for turning or extraction.

Bigger bins means materials, such as soil for sprinkling, need to be added in bigger quantities. So have a big bag of sieved soil or spent compost and a sack of ground lime standing nearby to sprinkle over each successive layer. Also have a storage butt for dirty water and ideally a hosepipe or rainwater butt too, as dryness is a bigger problem with larger bins where more of the wastes are likely to be tougher and drier.

It is possible with bigger bins that are rapidly filled to not remix, but this is strongly advised against. Obviously a bank of two or more is handy and allows materials to be moved from one to another easily and sequentially; so ripe compost may be being sieved from number 4, maturing in number 3, and cooking in number 2, having been just turned in from number 1, leaving number 1 empty to receive the next materials arriving. Once number 4 is empty the matured contents of number 3 are moved over and the semi-cooked contents of number 2 remixed into number 3 while the new materials from number 1 are mixed to cook in number 2, freeing up number 1 to receive the next batch again.

'More slats can be added as the contents rise, and a whole side can be removed for turning or extraction.'

Above left: The proper slatted bins have slats that slide in grooves in the uprights
Above right: Pallets can be tied at corners. Note extra timbers acting as insulation and increasing rigidity

Leaf-mould containers

Whereas for normal composting we mix a variety of materials, the autumn leaves are different. They break down but, when in any quantity, they take a long time and may slow a compost bin too much, so we often compost them on their own.

Containers can be made from wire netting attached to sturdy posts, either circular or square shapes work well. The leaves are bulky when fresh though they soon pack down – you may

use treading to pack them, as enough air will still be trapped between them. Ideally the leaves should be wetted as they're packed in. A roof is not necessary to keep off rain but it will stop the leaves blowing out again and cats adding their fertility to the invitingly soft top – a sheet of plastic will do if well weighted down.

It will take a couple of years for the leaves to turn to fine leaf-mould, which is superb when added to seed and potting composts or used as a soil enricher. If you don't want to use a container, you could just pack well-wetted leaves into large plastic bags, puncture them and hide them somewhere for a year or three. When you retrieve them they will be a quarter full of leaf-mould.

Above left: Well braced, corner of wire mesh leaf bin; **Above centre-left:** Plastic mesh cylinder works simply and easily; **Above centre-right:** Woven plastic bag does the job; **Above right:** Slatted bin with aeration gaps - proper job! Mind you, I would've set them upright

A light weekly clipping mulch about potatoes is less effort than earthing up, and even more effective

Grass clipping piles

Grass clippings are a perpetual problem in larger gardens, especially those lucky enough to have bowling greens, football or rugby pitches, tennis courts, etc! If the sward was to be rougher, as for an orchard, the clippings could be left in place or merely raked round trees and shrubs, however, with a requirement for neatness they need to be disposed of. (If contaminated with herbicides, the cuttings should only be used on grassed areas after composting.)

Grass clippings are one of the few cases of a material that is sufficiently active and finely divided so that a rotary composter may be of use and might give the mixing and aeration they need. Most ordinary bins will pack up if masses of clippings are added, unless they are intimately mixed with other materials. If piled into wire netting enclosures, as with leaves, you get apparent composting on the top and sides but in the anaerobic middle you get claggy, smelly, manure-like silage forming, which may endure for years. There may also be significant highly polluting run off.

Instead, alternate layers of fresh clippings with dry straw or shredded paper to allow air to enter sideways, as well as making a better mix. Add a sprinkling of soil to each layer and copious amounts of lime, unless the compost is destined for use on ericaceous lime-haters.

Turf mounds

When grass turves are available, say, when a lawn is lifted for a new bed, these should be composted separately not added en masse to a bin where they would slow the composting. Bits of turf are no problem, indeed are good material, it's the larger quantities we need to treat differently as we only want a partial breakdown. Turf can then be turned into a fantastic fibrous loam that's ideal for making or adding to seed and potting composts. Composted turves are the near-perfect material for growing melons and most other greenhouse crops, which would otherwise require a peat-based compost. The turves are stacked, upside down, and laid in alternating overlapping ways so as to hold together whilst forming a small mound or, better, (it has more air penetration) a wall. This then needs a roof (a weighed-down plastic sheet) to keep out light and shoot off rain but allow air inside. Old carpet, newspaper and cardboard can be used as insulation under the plastic and to stop any stray light getting in.

Unless the loam is intended for ericaceous plants, the turves should be lightly dusted with lime and/or blood, fish and bone meal as they're laid, which will speed the breakdown and make it sweeter and more suited as a potting or sowing compost. After six months or so, the grasses and any weeds die and wither away and the fibrous roots start to break down. Now it should be used; if it is left for more than a year or two it will become less active and will have lost more fibre. For potting, it's often best chopped to retain a coarse texture.

Slow bins and wildlife piles

These are best constructed on a larger scale and of wire netting, as for leaf-mould, as the material is often bulky. If more a wildlife pile than a bin, access for small critters will be required. The eventual dismantling and evacuation needs to be simple, so it will help future processing if the woody stuff is cut into short lengths. You could wet it daily with vile liquids (build in a plastic sheet or tray and a collection bottle to catch the run-through, which will be plenty) to encourage rough material to break down more quickly. This is not needed if the pile is more for wildlife, when a roof should also be fitted to exclude rain. For quicker composting, wet prospective slow materials with vile liquids then sprinkle them with soil, spent compost and a really rich activator, such as blood, fish and bone meal. Then layer these with grass clippings or stinging nettles, sprinkling lime on each layer and soil and lime on top. Finally, top the pile with an insulated plastic cover to keep the moisture in. When a year or two has passed, dig out and sieve the contents; most will have degraded but some bits will need picking out for the next bin.

'We tend to be a bit too tidy in our gardens, dead wood big and small is the niche for countless critters.'

Right: These prunings have been stacked neatly and tightly in a dry corner to act as a wildlife refuge

Hot boxes and hot beds

To create a hot compost heap, a plastic dalek bin can be given extra insulation, a dead refrigerator or freezer box recycled, or almost any bin given immense amounts of insulation. The idea is to retain all the heat given out by the composting materials, thus cooking them more effectively and quicker. In order to get air in, there has to be mixing and remixing, as for a plastic dalek. Several remixes are necessary to incorporate enough air to complete the process, but it is very quick and works well with small batches. The initial materials need to be finely divided and not too wet, as moisture will accumulate – serious quantities of manure or other activators help. The mix is loaded then the insulation reinforced. Remixing should be done after a week or so, usually adding more dry material such as straw, dead leaves or shredded paper at the same time to soak up excess moisture. Initially, some lime to soak up the gases should be added, but not much soil as this would slow down composting. After a second or third remix the compost is ready – within a month! It improves more if it is then stacked, covered and matured, dried and sieved. Even so, this can all be done in a third of the time of a conventional bin.

A proper hot bed is where the heat from composting lasts as long as possible. To achieve this, you need to include copious quantities of slow-to-break-down materials, such as fallen leaves and tanners' wastes (oak bark and leather scrapings) along with rapidly composting horse manure. By filling a large, suitable, solid-sided bin with layers of these or similar well-mixed materials several feet deep, the heat is given off over a month or two, then it's all remixed or replaced. A coating of lime and then a foot of soil to finish it off moderates the heat and removes noxious gases. A cold frame or similar on top creates a warm, moist micro-climate that is ideal for many crops and for use as a propagator for others. A good hot bed can be made in spring from grass clippings composted with equal quantities of spent compost and wetted shredded paper. This needs remixing every month or so when more clippings should be added. At the end of the season it's used as any other compost.

Pits and trenches

These are for the lazy with a vegetable plot or just a bit of spare ground. This method is anaerobic so it does not produce the same material as proper composting, but it works.

A pit, or the beginning of a trench, needs to be dug and the soil removed and kept to one side. Wastes should be added to the pit or hole, each layer has lime sprinkled on top and then some soil. Once the hole is full the rest of the soil is mounded on top, or the soil from the next hole or section of trench is put there. If wanted, in the first spring the mound can be used to grow marrow or squash family plants, sweet corn, or runner beans, the next spring the semi-decayed material underneath suits deep rooters such as brassicas, peas and beans, then follow up with potatoes, which help mix it up and break it down further. When the potatoes have gone, onions and then roots can follow, before starting another pit or trench on the same spot.

The marrow, courgette and squash family love to sit over rotting compost

Wormeries, snaileries or chickens...?

Above: A snailery - make the guilty work off their crime by giving us their manure
Right: A wormery can turn a profit if you sell them to anglers, and they are tasty snacks for your chickens

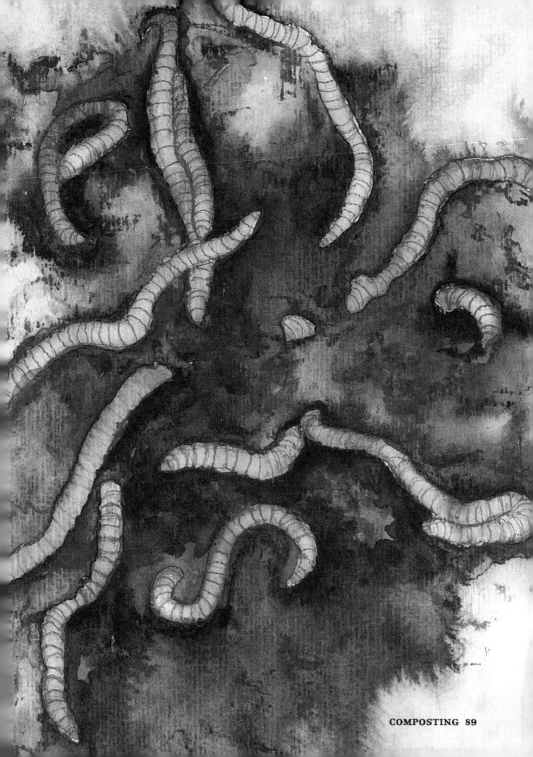

Wormeries

In a wormery, small red brandling worms chew up material and compost it inside themselves. A wormery the size of a dustbin can only handle very small amounts of material and will produce a revolting liquid that can be drained for use as a liquid feed. Every so often the bin should be emptied and the best stuff can then be removed for use as a potting compost additive or soil enricher and the worms and other stuff replaced to begin again.

You really do need two wormeries as once one is full, it takes many weeks before it's ready for emptying. A plastic dustbin or wheelie bin can be easily converted. Make a hole an inch or so above the base to drain into a receptacle placed to catch the run off, then insert a false bottom using something like plastic mesh supported on bars on bricks so the mass above can drain. Start the process with some partly rotted material and spent compost, making sure

Chop wastes up and make moist so the worms can work them more quickly

Worms will eventually turn the whole lot to a worm dropping manure

you include some red brandling worms. (These can be found by laying soaking wet cardboard sheets on the ground, and then a fortnight later when you pull back the sheets you can pick up the worms carefully.) Wastes should be added as they come, but preferably finely divided. With worms, meat and cheese are very acceptable, if added in small amounts and well chopped, as are most other kitchen and garden wastes – it's just they can't handle much at a time and it tends to get too wet, thus the need for drainage.

You need a lid to keep in smells and stop the worms leaving, too! Most commercially made wormeries are nearly sealed, however I find they work better if air holes are added at or above the liquid catchment zone in the bottom and also in the lid. Lime should not be added except in the most minute amounts, or as eggshells, as these worms prefer slightly acid conditions. In most ways a wormery is redundant if a usual compost bin can be used, however one may be useful in a flat or as a way of recycling meat and other such household wastes unsuited to composting, or as a precursor to composting.

Drainage in the bottom collects a liquid feed for dilution

One of the work force

Snaileries

These are much like wormeries but, instead, use snails to process wastes. Snaileries can be kept in well-ventilated containers – a plastic laundry basket is good. Give them water in the bottom, somewhere to live in broken pots, and feed them wastes so they will chomp away and produce snail droppings. When emptied out, this can be used to enrich potting composts and planting holes. Snails can get through a lot of green leafy material and a surprising amount of paper and cardboard; they also like eggshells and other sources of calcium for their shells. You could even farm them...

Left: Some consider this a potential delicacy
Right: Snails rasp their food into bits, and make a fibrous manure

Chickens

Chickens are not a composting method but are great pre-processors of wastes if these are spread on the ground for them. They will eat many vegetables and fruits, bugs and weed seeds and turn these into prime compost activator. This they spread over the uneaten stuff, which is scuffled and bruised by their claws. It really is a grand way to mix and prepare wastes, but you must exclude anything that has had contact with any animal products in the UK – however, if you live in a less deranged country you might see the advantages. Once a pile of compost has been cooked and matured, chickens could be allowed access to it; they will scratch it to bits, removing more seeds and bugs, and then it can be easily scooped, sieved and stored. You could even make special worm heaps (include lots of corrugated cardboard for worms) to turn over just to feed the hens.

Above left: A Silkie hen is small, compact and a good mother. She will diligently scratch all day
Above right: A cockerel is not essential unless you want fertile eggs
Right: They wear this path bare - it leads to where I feed them, of course!

What to do with your home-made compost

Use it. There is no point having piles of matured compost just sitting around; dig the stuff out and lavish it on your garden to feed the soil, crops and flowers. You can add huge quantities to almost any soil, as it will only make it more suitable for most plants. (Compost could conceivably be a tad too rich for some plants, such as hardy annual flowers, but it will still make them better protected against water stress). Although some may resent the weed seeds that inevitably escape composting, compost still makes a good mulch around trees, shrubs and soft fruit – all the better if it's sieved first. Compost can be used to fill the bottom half of planters, tubs and

even hanging baskets; again, it is better if it's sieved. Good sieved compost can even be used as potting compost, though the result will be less weedy if it is topped off with a layer of bought-in sterile compost. Garden compost is not very suitable as sowing compost for any but the biggest, toughest seeds, though it becomes more so if partly sterilised by steaming or microwaving.

What type of compost will you produce?

If different bins were made of different materials you'd think the result would be widely different, but in practice, with the usual varied mix of ingredients the result is remarkably uniform for most gardeners. Obviously, if all the materials you start with are totally lacking in some element then afterwards there can hardly be more. Although, of course, if you have especially collected proportionately many weeds containing some element or the other, then the material will be correspondingly richer, and if more soil was added, or less, it will vary a bit in texture or colour. If much lime was added the pH will be higher, and it may suit vegetables rather than ericaceous plants, but otherwise it will still be very much the same. As I said before, it is so much like rich fertile soil or bought-in potting compost that it seems hard to remember what compost comes from. If it's wet and claggy it merely needs to dry a little to be ready to sieve, but it could still be used as is mixed into planting holes.

Right: Not so much the factory floor as the power-house - this is where the best fertility and pest control are created

Sieving and storing

As mentioned earlier, it really is worth sieving compost; the result is so much more uniform, and so much more pleasant to handle. It's nicer to see when sticks, lumps, plastic bits and so on have been removed, and sieved compost breaks down even quicker than if it is just coarsely chopped.

The skill with sieving compost is to get it dryish but not totally dessicated. Chop the compost with a spade and then pass it through a coarse sieve with holes about a centimetre or half an

inch across. I have fitted a heavy metal sieve to my wheelbarrow so I can push compost straight through to move and store it elsewhere. The spoil should be picked over for bits of real trash that need evicting, such as plastic and metal. Stones need collecting for other uses while the rest of the larger unsiftable bits can be shot straight into the next bin as an inoculant.

Storing sieved compost in black bags or closed dustbins allows it to mellow a bit more, and it should always be brought under cover a week before use so it can warm up.

Soil enricher

Compost is the best soil enricher and is as good as, if not better than, well-rotted manure. After all, it is not animal-free, as it has plenty of droppings from the countless small animals and microbes we don't see.

It's best to apply compost to the topsoil and fork it in, where it incorporates naturally and quickly, rather than put it down the bottom of a trench. Only a few plants really appreciate coming across a discrete 'lump' or layer of compost underneath them, and which will slowly disappear, leaving a void. It's worth mixing compost into the soil when planting any perennial and some hungry annual crops, but more as a soil inoculant rather than as a replacement for the soil. If you give roots a hole full of pure compost they will be reluctant to leave, thus it's best intimately mixed with soil in as large a planting hole as possible. More compost is almost always better applied as a mulch rather than as a dense mass around the roots.

Compost tea

This can be used as diluted liquid extract to inoculate and enrich barren soils and rejuvenate tired potting composts. Sieved garden compost is packed into nylon tights or similar which are then tied up and immersed in a bucket or butt of rainwater. The resultant tea should be used as soon as possible, as the best microflora may 'drown' and the properties change as others take over. So this tea needs diluting down and adding to the next watering, not making and keeping. Plants in pots and containers are especially rejuvenated by this tea. Some people even spray it onto plants suffering pest and disease problems believing it has almost magical properties – science is now confirming that this is in fact the case.

Top left: Loading nylon stocking with sieved compost
Top right: Tying tea-stocking with some room for swelling
Bottom left: Lowering tea sock gently as it soaks up water
Bottom right: Gently swirling tea sock to percolate out extract

Mulch

Garden compost, especially raw, unsifted, claggy stuff, does not a pretty mulch make, but if it's dried, chopped and sieved then it looks fine. However, it is more active than most mulches, which means it disappears rapidly and needs constant topping up. Also, as it's not sterile, as with, say, composted bark, some weed seeds are likely to survive and cause aggravation. I personally do not mind this. Where compost is used around soft fruit, roses, shrubs and trees, grass-clipping mulches can be applied on top to 'cure' the weeds. Where compost is used as a mulch about vegetables, the weeds are dealt with during the usual cultivations – and hoed in weed seedlings are just more good food for the soil.

Left: Not the place for a weed seed infested compost top dressing, as sieved leaf-mould compost is better
Right: Here a top dressing of weed seed infested compost is fine

Potting composts

Sifted garden compost does not beat or replace the best commercial potting composts, but it is better by far than the worst. The trouble for any potting compost is it's one size has to fit all. So if you want to grow, say, tomatoes and petunias in your own or any other compost, it may well work, but not optimally, for one or the other, and is unlikely to work very well for both. So a simple solution is to experiment. Pot up several similar seedlings in slightly different mixes: one in proprietary compost, one in sifted compost, one in sifted compost plus a little extra lime, another with extra wood ashes and, say, one with fish meal and another with bone meal. In a few weeks you will see obvious differences and can adjust, accordingly, the bulk of the compost about to be used for potting up the rest of the plants.

Most sifted garden compost packs down if overwatered and may need some extra grit. As garden composts are usually somewhat weedy, they're best used to fill the bottom half or three-quarters of each pot or container, and the rest filled with a bought-in, sterile compost.

Right: Fill the bottom half with sieved garden compost to economise by all means but finish off with a more sterile commercial mix

Appendix

Mineral values of weeds

The weeds opposite are especially useful as mineral accumulators, so they may be encouraged for this reason, though some may potentially cause problems by over-wintering pests and diseases (marked*). In general, these are mostly easy to kill off and collect for compost whilst small, but some may become established and hard to eradicate if allowed to get larger. It is their very competitiveness for their preferred minerals that makes these weeds such bad companions but so good for compost. Weeds such as thornapple will scavenge scarce phosphates from a very poor soil and then, when composted and returned, will significantly increase their availability. However, if these weeds are left to ripen their seed the phosphates become locked up in the seeds and are then no longer available until germinated and gathered as new seedlings or plants.

Chickweed accumulates copper, iron, manganese, nitrogen, potassium.*

Chicory accumulates magnesium, potassium.

Clovers accumulate nitrogen.

Comfrey accumulates potassium.

Corn chamomile accumulates calcium, potassium.

Corn Marigold accumulates calcium, phosphorus.

Daisies accumulate calcium, magnesium.

Dandelion accumulates calcium, copper, iron, nitrogen.

Fat hen accumulates calcium, iron, nitrogen, phosphorus, potassium, sulphur.*

Foxgloves accumulate iron.

Goosegrass accumulates calcium, potassium.

Groundsel accumulates iron, nitrogen.*

Plantains accumulate cobalt, magnesium, potassium, silica.*

Purslane accumulates calcium, nitrogen, phosphorus, potassium, sulphur.

Salad burnet accumulates magnesium.

Scarlet pimpernel accumulates calcium.

Sheep's sorrel accumulates phosphorus.

Shepherd's purse accumulates calcium.*

Silverweed accumulates calcium, iron, magnesium.

Sowthistles accumulate copper, nitrogen.

Stinging nettles accumulate iron, silica.

Sun spurge accumulates boron.

Tansy accumulates potassium.

Thistles accumulate potassium.

Thornapple accumulates phosphorus, potassium.

Vetches accumulate cobalt, copper, nitrogen, phosphorus, potassium.

Yarrow accumulates copper, magnesium, nitrogen, phosphorus, potassium.

Index